I0172036

STEP FOUR - DISCIPLING FRUIT-PRODUCERS

TEACHER MANUAL

DR HENDRIK VORSTER

STEP FOUR - DISCIPLING FRUIT-PRODUCERS

-- Teacher Manual --

"Ephesians 4:12 (NIV)

"to equip his people for works of service, *so that the body of Christ may be built up..."*

Dr. Hendrik J Vorster

COPYRIGHT

Discipleship Foundations
Step 4 – Discipling Fruit-producers (Teacher Manual)
By Dr. Hendrik J. Vorster

A practical leadership guide to disciple fruit-producers.
Apart from this Handbook, you will also need the following items to complete your study:

A New International Version of the Bible.
A pen or pencil to write the answers.
Coloured pencils (red, blue, green and yellow).

For more copies and information please visit and write to us at: www.
churchplantinginstitute.com
resources@churchplantinginstitute.com

Copyright © churchplantingdoctor.com

All rights reserved.

No part of this publication may be reproduced, stored in a retrieval system, or transmitted in any form or by any means, electronic, mechanical, photocopying, recording or otherwise, without written permission from churchplantingdoctor.com

Scripture taken from the HOLY BIBLE,
New International Version
Copyright 1973, 1978, 1984, 2011 Biblica.
Used by permission of Zondervan.

Church Planting Doctor and the Church Planting Institute are Registered Ministries of Cornerstone Ministries International.

ISBN 13-978-1-7366426-0-3

1

INTRODUCTION

The *fourth phase of Discipleship* deals with us *bearing lasting Fruit* through *consistently putting into practice* what we've learnt, and by *living a life* of love, *worth following*, and *shepherding* those *entrusted* to *our care*.

This Step is all *about producing fruit* through *application of learnt experiences* and *Gift discovery and use*. I am always excited about this phase since it is always great to disciple obedient practitioners.

What sets the *next two steps* apart from previous steps in the *Discipleship Foundation Series* is that *these* two *Steps help you unlock* your *leadership abilities*, *sharpen* your intentional *focus* to stay on course with God's purpose on your life, and *establishes pilot lights* that will *keep you on course* to *a fruitful* and *multiplying life*.

Jesus taught about the importance of putting the Word into practice on a number of occasions. We should carry that same expectation in our hearts for our Disciples.

> *Matthew 7:24 (NIV)* "24 *Therefore everyone who hears these words of mine and puts them into practice is like a wise man who built his house on the rock.*'"

> *Luke 8:21 (NIV) "21 He replied, 'My mother and brothers are **those who hear God's word and put it into practice.'"***

At this stage of the journey your Disciples are more mature and diligent followers of the Lord Jesus. They are accountable in their walk with God and before men. Our role is to lead them to become purposeful Leaders, and we do that by addressing the following areas as we walk with them and ensure that they put God's Word into practice.

Discipler Note!

As Disciplers, our purpose is to facilitate ways in which our disciples can put the things we share, into practice. This process is marked by us continuing to share the Word of God into their lives, but then, instead of instructing them how to put it into practice, we require them to take action and share with us ways in which they anticipate putting it into practice. This process is deemed successful when they voluntarily and spontaneously give us regular feedback. It is in the extent to which they give us feedback and share with us, that we know with assurance, that they are growing and maturing. One of the signs of maturity is the practice of willing answerability.

> 1 Peter 3:15 (NIV)
> 15 But in your hearts revere Christ as Lord. ***Always be prepared to give an answer to everyone who asks you to give the reason for the hope that you have.*** But do this with gentleness and respect,

Your disciples will complete the action steps, at the end of each session. Take time during each following time together, to revisit the activities and action steps they took as a result of your previous time together. By a way of hearing "how they are going?" Determine what steps to take to ensure they "*observe everything*" we learn from the Word.

The successful outcome of our mission has been determined by the Lord Jesus, in that He commanded that we: *"teach them to obey [observe] everything I taught you."* The extent to which we see them willingly observe the things we teach them, is the extent to which they have become true Followers of Jesus Christ.

WALKING WITH PURPOSE

Finding one's purpose and living out the Purpose God designed you for, is most fulfilling. Romans 8 verse 28 says that we have been *"Called for a purpose."* That purpose is to make His Name known and to do the things God planned for us to do.

> *Romans 8:28 (NIV) "28 And we know that in all things God works for the good of those who love him, who have been **called according to his purpose.**"*

All of us have a deep desire to see that all things work out fine, regardless of what we are facing or going through. It is at this very point that we embrace this Scripture as a promise to us. However, when we read further, we see the conditional clarification to all of us who find ourselves affirming with a *"yes"* to *"those who love Him."* This conditional clarification determines that things will work out for good for those who *"have been called according to His purpose."* Some Believers do not generally see themselves as *"Called."* Most Believers actually think that it refers to Pastors and other more prominent Christian Leaders, however, as far as what you have included yourself in the promise and initial clarification of being one who "*love Him,*" you are included as one who "*have been called according to His purpose.*"

Definition of *purpose*

The word "Purpose" is defined by the online Merriam-Webster Dictionary as:

    1 a: something set up as an object or end to be attained : INTENTION

    b: RESOLUTION, DETERMINATION

    2: a subject under discussion or an action in course of execution.[1]

A key phrase that might best describe how we walk and fulfill our purpose, might be: "*living intentionally with determined resolution.*"

In our previous Step of our Discipleship Foundations Series we discovered and developed our Gifts and various skills for the purpose of using them. In a sense this "**discovering**" of our gifts and skills, is an awakening to uncover and discover the Anointing and Purpose God placed on our lives to advance His Kingdom.

In understanding the gifts He placed in us, and discovering the way in which He anointed us, we come to understand our purpose, or as it actually is: God's Purpose for our lives. I believe that God prepared things for us to do. He created us to do the things He gifted us for.

> *Ephesians 2:10 (NIV) "10 For we are God's handiwork, created in*
> *Christ Jesus **to do good works, which God prepared in advance***
> *for us to do."*

Our maturity is determined by both our *willingness* and <u>*obedience*</u> to serve the purpose and will of God, as well as *our acceptance of* <u>*responsibility*</u> for the outcome we desire.

How do I walk with purpose?

- Discover your spiritual gifts. Know and understand how God anointed you.
- Commit to actively pursue ways in which you could avail yourself to be used by God to build up the church. Use the Gifts in various scenarios.
- Become focused and intentional in flowing in the Power of the Holy Spirit.
- Look for ways in which you could build people up, especially by the power of the Holy Spirit.
- Our primary purpose is to seek and save the lost.
- We live to worship God, in song, in life and through our example.
- We also live to put into practice the gifts and skills He gave us.

I pray that you will show your maturity in Christ by your consistent use of what God built inside of you.

*Hebrews 5:14 (NIV) "14 But solid food is **for the mature, who by constant use have trained themselves** to distinguish good from evil."*

Action Steps

1. List the three most prominent Gifts.

_____

_____

_____

2. Name three opportunities you will pursue to use your Gifts to build up the church. I commit to:

_____

_____

_____

3. Share one way in which you experienced how the Holy Spirit used you during the last week.

_____

_____

_____

4. Share how you saw the Gifts in operation in your life this week.

_____

_____

_____

5. In which circumstances have you experienced a greater move of the Holy Spirit in your life this week?

_____

_____

_____

6. In which way were you most effective in **seeking and saving** lost people?

_____

_____

_____

7. In which way did you practice "constant use" in your life this week?

_____

_____

_____

3

BUILD PURPOSEFUL RELATIONSHIPS

The second area that we focus on is to keep our Disciples focused on building purposeful relationships. It is important to constantly keep your Disciples focused, and one of those key areas is to keep them focused on is souls, and more specifically on finding the most "*worthy men and woman*" they can find to advance the Kingdom of God. We need to reach the lost regardless of the cost.

John Maxwell says: "*Everything rises and falls on Leadership*"

I humbly submit "*Growing a healthy Church rises and falls on how effective we are at making <u>Disciples</u>*." The quality of the Disciples we make, will determine the impact their lives will have on others around them.

The extent to which you will be able to make Disciples is the extent to which your church will grow in a healthy way.

Disciples are those men and woman where your Peace finds rest in their hearts.

You know that you have found a Disciple when they, out of their own free will, express a desire that you help them grow in their faith, however, even then, be wise in who you Disciple. *Build the strongest team* that *you are able to lead* for the Lord Jesus.

The Lord Jesus set the example.

The Lord **Jesus set a pattern and model** when He **started His ministry** on earth, **by whom He chose** to be His Disciples. **He chose worthy men** to disciple. Even though Jesus declared in Luke 4 verse 18 that the *"Spirit of the Lord is upon me to preach the Good News to the Poor,"* He never started His Discipling ministry with the poor, He started His ministry with "Worthy men."

Jesus started His Discipling ministry with "Worthy men."

We see Jesus' strategy, clearly modelled to us, in the Gospel of Luke. One Day He was preaching to crowds of people next to the Lake of Gennesaret. This is what the Bible teaches us in Luke chapter five.

> *Luke 5:1 (NIV) "One day as Jesus was standing by the Lake of Gennesaret, the people were crowding around him and listening to the word of God."*

While He was preaching, He saw at the water's edge two boats, and got into the one *"belonging"* to Simon Peter. He went into the water just enough so that everyone could hear and see Him, and he continued to teach the people.

> *Luke 5:3 (NIV) "3 He got into one of the boats, the one belonging to Simon, and asked him to put out a little from shore. Then he sat down and taught the people from the boat."*

When Jesus had finished speaking to the crowd, He asked Simon Peter to *"put out into the deep water, and let down your nets for a catch."*

Luke 5:4 (NIV) "When he had finished speaking, he said to Simon, 'Put out into deep water, and let down the nets for a catch.'"

Peter was resistant at first, since they spent the whole night out on the waters without success, yet at Jesus' insistence he conceded and let down his nets into the deep water. What followed was amazing, Peter hauled such a large school of fish that they had to call over **their partners** in the other boat to help bring in the fish.

Peter was amazed, realizing that he just observed a miracle. He fell at Jesus' feet and begged for His forgiveness.

Luke 5:8-9 (NIV) "8 When Simon Peter saw this, he fell at Jesus' knees and said, "Go away from me, Lord; I am a sinful man!" 9 For he and all his companions were astonished at the catch of fish they had taken,"

Jesus call Peter, Andrew, James and John to follow Him

It was at this juncture that Jesus called these Fisherman to follow Him. You see, Peter was not just a Fisherman, no, he was the owner of a fishing boat, and if we read the whole portion of Scripture, we see that he had a crew, called companions, as well as partners, James and John.

> Luke 5:9-11 (NIV) For he and all his companions were astonished at the catch of fish they had taken, 10 and so were **James and John**, the sons of Zebedee, **Simon's partners.**
> Then Jesus said to Simon, "*Don't be afraid; from now on you will fish for people.*" 11 **So they** pulled their boats up on shore, *left everything and followed him.*

Just think about it for a moment. "*How many people do you know who own their own boat?*" Not many, I guess. Why? The answer is simple: "*boats are expensive.*" Can you imagine owning a boat 2000 years ago? I think that you will agree, these first Disciples were "**Worthy men.**"

Jesus call Levi to follow Him.

The Gospel of Luke also tells us that Jesus then went past the Tax booth of Levi and called him to follow Him.

> *Luke 5:27-28 (NIV) "27 After this, Jesus went out and saw a tax collector by the name of Levi sitting at his tax booth. "Follow me," Jesus said to him, 28 and Levi got up, left everything and followed him."*

In those days the Tax Collectors were like the wealthiest people around, not necessarily by honest decree, but wealthy indeed. They were like Bankers who rolled in the money. *Levi was a "Worthy man."*

We know from Colossians 4 verse 14 that *Luke was a doctor.* A doctor is regarded as a "**worthy**" person in our day. How much more would they have been regarded as a "Worthy" men, 2000 years ago? We also know that **Judas** *handled the money*, hence we could assume that he was a worthy man as well, who could be trusted with the Lord's finances.

What we can see clearly, is that these disciples were all regarded as worthy men in their day. Being *commercial Fishermen, a Tax Collector, a Governor of a Roman Province, an Accountant, and a Doctor, these men were all <u>worthy</u> men.*

Jesus taught His Disciples the principle of starting with "Worthy" men and woman.

When Jesus sent His Disciples to go and preach the Gospel, He gave them this same wonderful strategy. I believe this strategy will serve us well in finding our disciples.

Matthew 10:11-13 (NIV) "11 Whatever town or village you enter,
search there for some worthy person and stay at their house
until you leave. 12 As you enter the home, give it your greeting.
13 If the home is deserving, let your peace rest on it; if it is not,
let your peace return to you."

Finding a Worthy man, a House of Peace or a Man of Peace in the town, suburb or place **where God called** you to extend His Kingdom, **is essential.** These are the "worthy" people through whom the Gospel message will be advanced. Always look for the worthiest people who could, and would, take the message you bring to them, further.

A "Worthy Man" defined.

- **A Worthy man is defined as being a person of <u>worth</u>.**

Their worth can relate to their **monetary substance**, but not necessarily. Most worthy people are counted as worthy because of the **Leadership positions** they hold in government, business, organisations and society at large. Worthy people are mostly counted as worthy because of their **influence and connectedness.** They are counted as worthy because of their **decision-making powers.** Their ability to make influential decisions, which could potentially impact thousands, make them worthy and powerful.

- **Worthy people are <u>visionary</u>.**

They are the **people who love to be involved** with **people who have a vision**. The only vision poor people have, normally relates to what you have on offer for them, whereas worthy people **will help you fulfill the vision** God gave you. If you share a vision with worthy people, they will frequently ask and offer their help to see that vision fulfilled.

- Worthy people are people who take **action** and **take responsibility.**

One of the *outstanding characteristics of "Worthy People"* is the level to which *they assume and take responsibility.* They are quite satisfied to let *the buck stop with them*, since they know what is required to get the job done. You would be wise to ask God for "Worthy" men and woman to start your new ministry with.

- A *"worthy man"* could be a man or a woman or a couple.

Worthy people are not defined by their sex, race or education. We have examples of both men and woman who led churches in New Testament times, like a *Lydia* in Philippi. *Pricilla and Aquila* were those worthy people in Paul's life.

- A worthy man is someone who runs his or her own business, small or large, or manages, or leads a business, organization or industry.

Wherever you travel around the world, regardless of how prosperous or impoverished nations are, you will find worthy people. They are the people who step out in faith, hope and much perseverance to start their little business, where they see an opportunity to meet a need in the market. From *buying and selling fruit and vegetables* along the road to setting up a little shop where local people can buy *bread and milk*, these people start a business. They could be the *mechanic* down the road, *welder* who manufactures gates and security screens, a *Builder*, a *Carpenter*, a *Salesperson*, to more known *business entrepreneurs* into well-known commercial enterprises.

Unfortunately many people think that in the absence of the latter, the former do not count as worthy. I have seen How most of the generosity to advance the Gospel, come from those who were not generally deemed as worthy. We love people who take initiative, step out in faith, and build something that will not only benefit themselves, but provide an income and security for people around them.

My insistence on finding worthy people should not just be dismissed as impossible within your area, village, town, city or nation, since your eyes have never been opened to look for them. *There are worthy people everywhere*. Through their perseverance and faith they provide for their own families, but most of the time, *they become the source for help* to many others, less fortunate than them. **These are people of worth.**

- **A worthy man could be the principle or department head of a School, College or Educational institution.**

In most countries of the world, those who hold *positions in education*, are *regarded as worthy* people. I belief they are some of the *most influential people* on the planet because of their advantaged *position to influence* their captive audience in an undisturbed and non-coerced way. Pray that God will bless you with worthy educators to disciple.

- The worthy man **is distinguished by their stand, reputation and stature** in the community.

The Apostle Paul practiced it in his Church Planting ministry.

The Apostle Paul, when he **planted the church in Philippi**, founded the church on *practicing this very principle*. You will recall that he had this "Macedonian Call" and straightaway went to the region of Macedonia to preach the Word of God there. Acts 16 verses 12-15 tell us this amazing affirmative story of this principle being applied.

> *Acts 16:12-15 (NIV) From there we traveled to Philippi, a Roman colony and the leading city of that district of Macedonia. And we stayed there several days. 13 On the Sabbath we went outside the city gate to the river, where we expected to find a place of prayer. We sat down and began to speak to the*

women who had gathered there. 14 One of those listening was a
*woman from the city of Thyatira named **Lydia, a dealer in***
purple cloth. *She was a worshiper of God. **The Lord opened her***
heart to respond to Paul's message. *15 When she and the*
members of her household were baptized, she invited us to her
*home. **"If you consider me a believer in the Lord,"** she said,*
***"come and stay at my house."** And **she persuaded us.**"*

We see that it was here that he met a *"Worthy Woman"* called
Lydia, she was *a Trader in purple cloth.* We also see that *she had*
authority, since *she was able to persuade* Paul and his companions to
stay at her house. She invited them to her house, where they stayed
until the church was established.

Priscilla and Aquila

Another example came from when **Paul planted the church in**
Corinth. He met a "**Worthy Man and Woman**" called **Pricilla and**
Aquila. Aquila was a tentmaker like he was. Once he found this
"Worthy Man" he stayed with them and from there the Church grew.

> *Acts 18:1-3 (NIV) "[18:1] After this, Paul left Athens and went to*
> ***Corinth.** [2] **There he met a Jew named Aquila,** a native of*
> *Pontus, who had recently come from Italy with **his wife***
> ***Priscilla**, because Claudius had ordered all the Jews to leave*
> *Rome. Paul went to see them, [3] and because **he was a***
> ***tentmaker** as they were, **he stayed and worked with them.**"*

The Apostle Paul also passed this Principle on to Timothy.

Interestingly, and most noteworthy for us, is the fact that the Apostle
Paul gave this same advice to his disciple, and spiritual son, Timothy.

> *2 Timothy 2:2 (NIV) "2 And the things you have heard me say in the presence of many witnesses **entrust to <u>reliable</u> people who will also be qualified to teach others."***

In 2 Timothy 2 verse 2 we read that he advised Timothy to *"entrust"* the things he was taught *"to <u>reliable</u> people."* Paul instructed him to entrust the things he learnt and observed from Paul, to reliable people who will be ***able to <u>teach</u> others.***

One of the essentials of discipleship, is starting with the right people. ***Worthy and reliable people*** need to be ***your first disciples.*** If you truly follow the example that the Lord set for us, you too will establish a work that will last long after you are gone to be with the Lord. Starting your ministry with **the <u>right</u> people will ensure fruitfulness** and **multiplication.**

Most Pastors I speak to **have this dream** of having a huge ***disciple-making ministry*** that would see **spiritual sons and daughters** multiply their work, however, few see their dreams realised as they are surrounded with the wrong caliber of people. ***To fulfill such a noble vision and dream; you need to be surrounded by the worthiest people*** that you are able to find and lead.

Where do we find these "Worthy Men" to be our Disciples?

Worthy people are everywhere, but more so where we intentionally pray for them. In the very famous chapter 29 of Jeremiah, we learn a powerful principle to practice this principle of finding and discipling worthy men.

> Jeremiah 29:7 (NIV) 7 Also, ***seek the peace and prosperity of the city*** to which I have carried you into exile. ***Pray to the LORD*** for it, because **if it prospers, you too will prosper."**

Through this Scripture we learn that God desire that we 1.) *"seek the peace and prosperity of the city"* to which He called us, and 2.) That as we pray for its prosperity, that when it prospers, we too will prosper.

God wants us to pray for the peace and *prosperity* of the village, town, city and Nation where He called us to make disciples for Him. In the context of this session, it means that *we pray for the prosperity of every business* in the place *where we live and work.* I found that the more intentional we are in prayer, by praying for businesses and business leaders, God allows us to make divine connections with them, and He starts to speak to us about their circumstances.

When Jesus walked into Peter's life, there was a divine encounter. *Peter's life was changed* because of *Jesus' engaging with him.* As we walk through our neighbourhoods and pray for and over the businesses, we too will experience this kind of divine encounters. *Pray for the worthiest people you can lead to Christ* and *walk expectantly* for the time that you will have that divine moment with them to *lead them to Christ.* These *divine encounters* often provide an *opportunity* for us to flow in the *Gifts of the Holy Spirit* and touch lives in a powerful way. *Seek God* for such *divine connections* to *connect you* with the *worthiest people He prepared* for you *to disciple.*

We could find these "worthy men" in two primary areas:

1. **Home** church. They could be those whom God gives you right from the start from within your current Church, such as was the situation with the Apostles Paul and Barnabas in the Church in Antioch when the Holy Spirit called them to go out on their first Missionary journey. We read this amazing story in Acts 13 verses 1-5.

2. **Mission field.** These disciples could be found whilst sharing the Gospel among those who come to the Lord through the preaching of the Word such as what we find in Acts 16 verses 12 to 15 or Acts 19 verses 1-12. They could be those business people you pray for in your community.

Fast and pray before you call "worthy men" as your Disciples.

This process of finding and choosing disciples always starts with a season of **Fasting and Prayer**. Jesus spent a night praying before He chose His Disciples. God chose Paul and Barnabas during a time of Fasting and Prayer in the church in Antioch.

The process of finding your disciples might take you *three to nine months*. It will require some serious *focus, diligence and efficiency*. It is far better to start a new ministry with people whom you led to the Lord and show a strong commitment to be discipled by you, than attempting to "*pour new wine into old wineskins." New believers are easier to lead and disciple.*

I remember, before I met my wife, I always wondered how I will know, and then when it happens, you know. Well, for those of you who have been blessed to be married to a wonderful man or woman of God will know what I am talking about.

Well, the reason for my brief divergence is this:

"Ask God for His choice of Disciples for you."

Rather *focus your attention* on *finding your twelve* than running after every proverbial "*Tom, Dick or a Harry*," who does *not want to follow, learn* or *put the Word of God into practice.*

The Church of Jesus Christ *would be so much stronger* and *larger if we spent* our energies on *prayer* and earnest *pursuit of those who God chose for us* to *Disciple.*

May we always carry the Great Commission close to our hearts, and with wisdom *choose* and make *the best Disciples* we are *able to lead.*

*Matthew 28:19 (NIV) "19 Therefore **go and make disciples** of all nations, **baptizing them** in the name of the Father and of the Son and of the Holy Spirit, 20 and **teaching them to obey everything** I have commanded you. And surely, I am with you always, to the very end of the age."*

As you go, seek and save the Lost, and teach them to observe everything the Lord taught you and remember to choose men who will be able to teach others.

Action Steps

1. Record the Names of the twelve worthiest people you know in your local community, who will be able to teach other. Before you record their names, consider: your access to them, your faith and confidence to lead them to Christ, and ultimately your ability to disciple them. Now, prayerfully record those names as they come to mind.

_____

_____

_____

_____

_____

_____

_____

_____

_____

_____

_____

_____

2. Pray for these twelve people until they come to know Christ as Lord.

3. Pray for the peace and prosperity of these worthy people in their businesses or fields of leadership.

4. Pray that God will connect you with the disciples He chose for you to disciple.

5. Make a list of three worthy people, from the list above, whom you will intentionally pursue to build a purposeful relationships with.

_____

_____

_____

PRAYING EFFECTIVELY

Priesthood.

During this phase of Discipleship, we take deeper steps in our walk with God by learning what it means to be a Biblical, *New Testament Priest*. Thus far we primarily learned and practiced personal prayer, but that is not all that God planned for us in regard to prayer. God desires that we serve as His *"Holy Priests."* Priesthood is really about praying effectively, especially as it relates to us praying for others.

> *Revelation 1:5-6 (NIV) "5 ...To him who loves us and has freed us from our sins by his blood, 6 and **has made us to be** a kingdom and **priests to serve his God and Father**—to him be glory and power for ever and ever! Amen."*

Key Functions

One of the *key functions of a Priest* is to make *intercession* on behalf of others, especially those entrusted to our spiritual care.

God desires that we as Believers be a Kingdom of Priests, a Holy Priesthood. The Apostle Peter said in his Pastoral Epistle that God desires that we *"be built up in Him"* to be a spiritual house, *"to be a holy Priesthood."*

> 1 Peter 2:4-5 (NIV) 4 *As you come to him*, the living Stone — rejected by humans but chosen by God and precious to him— 5 you also, like living stones, are *being built into a spiritual house* to be *a holy priesthood, offering spiritual sacrifices* acceptable to God through Jesus Christ.

> 1 Peter 2:9 (NIV) 9 But you are a chosen people, *a royal priesthood*, a holy nation, God's special possession, that you may declare the praises of him who called you out of darkness into his wonderful light.

This is that time in our discipleship journey where we are *"being built to become a spiritual house to be a holy priesthood."* During this phase we take time to learn how to pray more effectively and efficiently on behalf of those the Lord desires us to reach, as well as those whom the Lord entrusted to us already. Through this process *we develop our prayer lives* into becoming *a Holy Priesthood.*

Melchizedek

The first priest we learn of in the Bible was Melchizedek. He was also the king of Salem.

> *Genesis 14:18-19 (NIV) "18 Then **Melchizedek** king of Salem brought out bread and wine. He was **priest of God Most High**, 19 and he blessed Abram, saying, "Blessed be Abram by God Most High, Creator of heaven and earth. And praise be to God Most High, who delivered your enemies into your hand." Then Abram gave him a tenth of everything."*

What we learn from this first encounter with a Priest is that He served Abraham with *"bread and wine"*, symbolic of serving him with *communion*; and *he blessed Abraham*; and *Abraham gave him a tenth* of everything.

- The Priest served communion
- He blessed the people, and
- He received the tithe.

Aaronic Priesthood

The second major encounter where we read about priests in the Bible, is in reference to where God instructed Moses to *set aside Aaron to serve as a Priest*, and his sons alongside him.

> *Exodus 40:12-15 (NIV) "12 **Bring Aaron** and **his sons** to the entrance to the tent of meeting and wash them with water. 13 Then **dress Aaron in the sacred garments, anoint him** and **consecrate him** so he may **serve me as priest**. 14 **Bring his sons** and dress them in tunics. 15 **Anoint them** just as you anointed their father, so **they may serve me as priests**. Their anointing will be to a priesthood that will continue throughout their generations."*

God wanted to dwell among His people and therefor instructed Moses to *build a Tabernacle*, according to a pattern He provided. Once Moses built the Tabernacle, God instructed him to set aside Aaron and his sons to serve in the Tabernacle as priests.

Functions of a Priest

The functions of a priest, as we learnt from the instructions of Moses, are manifold:

- **They provide fire and wood for the altar.**

> *Leviticus 1:7 (NIV) "7 The sons of Aaron, **the priest, are to put fire on the altar** and arrange wood on the fire."*

The Priests kept the fire on the altar burning. In a similar way, we are called on to keep the flame of the Gospel burning brightly as we consistently share the Good News of Jesus wherever we go.

We also *keep the fire burning in our lives* by *maintaining a vibrant relationship with God* through our *daily worship* of Him, *reading the Word, meditating and praying.* Our *spiritual disciplines* might be said to *represent the wood* through which we *keep our relationship on fire* and alive at the *Altar of Worship.*

The Lord spoke to the Angel of the Church in Laodicea, and warned them against lukewarmness. We similarly need to take heed to this warning and constantly *keep the fire of God burning brightly in our lives.*

> Revelation 3:15-16 (NIV) 5 I know your deeds, that you are neither cold nor hot. I wish you were either one or the other! 16 So, *because you are lukewarm*—neither hot nor cold—I am about to spit you out of my mouth.

One things *Priests do* is that they *keep the fervor of God ablaze*, both in their own lives, as well as in those around them. One of the ways in which we can *constantly assess* the fervency in lives is *through* our commitment and prevailing in prayer.

- **They serve in the Sanctuary and worship at the Altar daily.**

> *Numbers 18:2 (NIV) "2 Bring your fellow Levites from your ancestral tribe to join you and assist you when **you and your sons minister before the tent** of the covenant law."*

> *Numbers 18:5 (NIV) "5 You are to be responsible for the care of the sanctuary and the altar, so that my wrath will not fall on the Israelites again."*

Two things stand out in these two verse *about the function* of a

Priest: **Priests <u>minister</u> to the Lord daily** and they <u>Serve</u> by **taking care** of **all the responsibilities of the Sanctuary**. This also addresses how we take care of the sanctuary we keep for God in our lives.

> 1 Corinthians 6:19-20 (NIV) 19 Do you not know that your bodies are **temples of the Holy Spirit**, who is in you, whom you have received from God? You are not your own; 20 you were bought at a price. Therefore **honor God with your bodies**.

Sanctifying the Sanctuary.

This speaks to us about our attendance to **the place God has in our lives**. The extent to which we attend to keeping the sanctuary of God in our own lives, where the Spirit of the Living God lives, is the extent to which we will probably serve to keep the Sanctuary where the Church meet together, cared for. One way in which we keep the sanctuary of the Holy Spirit clean in our lives is by allowing the Holy Spirit to work His Sanctification work in us.

> 1 Peter 3:15 (KJV) 15 But <u>sanctify</u> the Lord God in your hearts: and be ready always to give an answer to every man that asketh you a reason of the hope that is in you with meekness and fear:

Constantly allowing the **sanctifying work** of the **Holy Spirit** and keeping Him **actively engaged** in our lives is **essential** to **maintaining the Presence** and **Power of God**.

- **They were to hear the confession of the sins of the people, and then bring the sacrifice for their sins to the altar.**

> *Leviticus 5:5-6 (NIV) "5 when anyone becomes aware that they are guilty in any of these matters, **they must confess in what way***

they have sinned. *6 As a penalty for the sin they have committed,* **they must bring to the LORD** *a female lamb or goat from the flock as* **a sin offering; and the priest shall make atonement for them for their sin."*

What we learn through this Mosaic Law, is the requirement of God that sinners confess their sins, as well as bring a sin offering to the Priest to make atonement for their sin. The Bible continues to describe the Priestly role in defining that it is their responsibility to bear the offences of the people. What that means is that they were responsible to God to appropriately deal with the pardoning of the sins of the people by offering these sin offerings, and by making atonement for them. In effect it was to hear and receive their confession and sacrifice, and then to pardon or forgive them.

Numbers 18:1 (NIV) Duties of Priests and Levites "1 The LORD said to Aaron, 'You, your sons and your family **are to bear the responsibility for offenses** *connected with the sanctuary, and you and your sons alone* **are to bear the responsibility for offenses connected with the priesthood.'"*

So many people struggle with the guilt of sin, not feeling that they have received forgiveness for their sins. So, often I see how our teaching on Christ's forgiveness, or simply saying to them that they are forgiven, releases them. The more we step into our Priestly role, the more we will see the impact it has on those around us when we 1. Intercede on their behalf, like Job did for his family's sins, and 2. Hear the confession of sins, and 3. Declare over them that Christ forgave them. In Him we have redemption and the forgiveness of our sins. This is also what Hebrews chapter five teaches.

Hebrews 5:1 (NIV) "Every high priest is selected from among the people and is **appointed to represent the people** *in matters related to God,* **to offer gifts and sacrifices for sins.**

We are called to represent people and offer intercession on their behalf. In a sense it is to stand in the gap for them before God.

> 1 Timothy 2:1-4 (NIV) 1 I urge, then, first of all, that petitions, prayers, *intercession* and thanksgiving *be made for all people* — 2 for kings and all those in authority, that we may live peaceful and quiet lives in all godliness and holiness. 3 This is good, and *pleases God our Savior, 4 who wants all people to be saved* and to come to a knowledge of the truth.

- **They deal gently with those who go astray and are weak in their faith.**

> *Hebrews 5:2 (NIV) "2 He is able to deal gently with those who are ignorant and are going astray, since he himself is subject to weakness."*

One of the *signs of those who pray* and *intercede for others*, is the *compassionate care* and *forbearance they apply* in those relationships. *We are called to deal gently* with those who are *ignorant* and are *going astray.*

- **They became priests in response to the Call of God to such service.**

> *Hebrews 5:4 (NIV) "4 And no one takes this honor on himself, but he receives it when called by God, just as Aaron was."*

In the same way as what we respond to the call of God to Salvation, we respond to His Call upon our lives to become His Priests. It is a Holy Calling, and as people respond to this call to become that Kingdom of Priests who would serve the Lord, and the people, we see the depth level increase in their lives, and the life of the Church.

Revelation 1:5-6 (NIV) 5 and from *Jesus Christ*, who is the faithful witness, the firstborn from the dead, and the ruler of the kings of the earth.

To him who loves us and has freed us from our sins by his blood, 6 and **has made us to be a kingdom and priests** to serve his God and Father —to him be glory and power for ever and ever! Amen.

To this have we been called, to be a kingdom of priests.

- **They addressed and encouraged those who went out into battle prior to them going into battle.**

*Deuteronomy 20:2-3 (NIV) "2 When you are about to go into battle, **the priest shall come forward and address the army. 3 He shall** say: 'Hear, Israel: Today you are going into battle against your enemies. **Do not be fainthearted or afraid; do not panic or be terrified by them.'"***

Before the army of Israel, or Judah, would go into any battle, they would first have the priest address them and pray for them. I have seen so many times, prior to engaging in business transactions and deals, that when two believers practice their priestly roles together that the Lord truly go before them and grant them success into whatever is at hand.

Conclusion

I pray that you will truly respond to the Call of God on your life to step up into His Call upon your life to serve as a Priest in His House. This is not a positional appointment in a local church, as some denominations have the custom of introducing, no, this is before you and God. We serve before Him, and as we serve He will reward us by answering our prayers and petitions.

I believe you are at this stage of your discipling journey because you have a sincere sense of the Call of God on your life to extend His Kingdom, and to serve His followers better. No serving in the Kingdom *bears as much fruit* as through those who encounter the Presence of God frequently, and *for more than just themselves.*

The more we delight ourselves in the Presence of the Lord, and then make intercession before God on behalf of others, we will see *the world around us change and transform* into *what He purposed* and *planned* before the Foundation of the world.

Action steps

1. Consciously and *verbally* accept the Call of God to become a Priest in the Household of God.
2. *Consecrate* yourself before God to serve as His Priest in His Sanctuary.
3. Set aside time, *daily*, to worship the Lord.
4. Make a list of people whom you are trusting the Lord for to be *Saved*. A shortlist of the *top three* always seem to be most effective in seeing them saved. 1 Timothy 2 verse 1 and 3 to 4.
5. *Make a list* of people in *high authority* for whom you will commit to *pray and intercede* for *regularly*. 1 Timothy 2 verse 2.
6. *Make a list* of *businesses and businesspeople* in your community or city for whom you will *commit to pray and intercede for* on a regular basis. Jeremiah 29 verse 7.
7. Set aside *extendable time to make intercession* for people *after a good time of soaking* in the Presence of God.
8. Be a *peacemaker*.
9. *Have a tender heart* towards *those who fail* and *fall* around you.
10. *Show kindness* to *those who confess their sins*.
11. *Be a reconciling forgiver*. Pardon people. Be gracious towards all men.

5

CARING COMPASSIONATELY

I t is such *an honour* to *be entrusted with* one of the precious *sheep in God's fold.* Our gratitude is shown in the way in which we care for those entrusted to our care.

In this session we revisit and remind ourselves of how to be a *"Good Shepherd."* Every man of God carries this care in their hearts for God's people. We need to both model compassionate care as well as teach our Disciples to care for those whom the Lord entrusted to them.

This session serves also as a reminder to *consistently apply* two *Kingdom Values*, namely "**Compassion**" and "**Caring.**" By caring compassionately, we combine our compassion with care.

There is a saying:

> *"People don't care how much you <u>know</u> until they know how much you <u>care</u>."*

The compassion you apply to your care makes the difference between providing care and *caring compassionately*. The first is done out of duty and the latter as *an expression of love*. The care we provide is felt more, and deeply appreciated, according to the measure of compassion we apply to our care.

Compassion

Compassion is the *feeling of* <u>*concern*</u>*, sorrow or pity* for someone, and *expressed* by *showing them kindness,* <u>*mercy*</u>*, sympathy or tenderness.* The Apostle Peter encouraged the Believers to practice compassion towards one another.

> *1 Peter 3:8 "Finally, be ye all of one mind, **having** <u>**compassion**</u> **one of** **another**, love as brethren, **be pitiful, be courteous**"*

Peter exhorts the Believers to *have compassion*, alongside *love* for the brothers, *being pitiful* and *courteous*. Out of the overflow of our understanding and appreciation of the Nature of God, we practice compassion. *The Word of God teaches* us that *God is a Compassionate God*, who is *full of mercy and Grace*.

> *Exodus 33:19 (NIV) "19 And the Lord said, 'I will cause all my* *goodness to pass in front of you, and I will proclaim my name,* *the Lord, in your presence. **I will have mercy on whom I will** **have mercy, and I will have compassion on whom I will have** **compassion.**'"*

What we learn here about *the Nature of God* is that He is truly a Compassionate God. Throughout Scripture this Value and Characteristic is mentioned.

> *Psalms 116:5 (NIV) "5 The Lord is gracious and righteous; **our God*** ***is*** <u>***full***</u> ***of compassion**."*

God is not just a compassionate God; *He is full of grace and compassion*. It is His desire that we practice compassion and care in our daily dealings with one another.

Exodus 22:26-27 (NIV) "26 If you take your neighbour's` cloak as a
pledge, return it by sunset, 27 because that cloak is the only
covering your neighbour has. What else can they sleep in?
*When they cry out to me, I will hear, **for I am compassionate**."*

*Psalms 86:15 (NIV) "15 But you, **Lord, are a compassionate and***
***gracious God**, slow to anger, abounding in love and*
faithfulness."

Colossians 3:12 (NIV) "12 Therefore, as God's chosen people, holy
*and dearly loved, **clothe yourselves with compassion**, kindness,*
humility, gentleness and patience."

What we learnt about **the Nature** and **Character of God** from the
beginning was His **great Compassion for His people.** On numerous
occasions we see His love and Compassion expressed towards His
people.

Compassion is the **show of sympathy, concern** and **empathy** towards
others **in their distress or shortcomings.** To be Compassionate is being
kind-hearted and **concerned, with care,** for those around us. Compassion is **showing consideration for the needs** and care of others.

Jesus told His Disciples this parable of **the Good Samaritan.** The
message of this Parable was clear; we need to show compassionate
care to our **"neighbour."** The way we show that we **love our neighbour**
is by practicing and **showing them compassionate care.**

We can see this compassionate care in the **life of Christ** expressed
towards people on a number of occasions. He expressed it when **He**
observed that they were **like sheep without a Shepherd.** He had compassion on the people when they were with Him for a few days without
eating. He was concerned for their welfare.

Matthew 9:36 (NIV) "36 When he saw the crowds, he had
***compassion on them,** because they were harassed and helpless,*
like sheep without a shepherd."

On a number of occasions, He fed the people out of concern for their welfare. In the Apostle Paul's address to the Church in Philippi he exhorted them, through their union with Christ, to be *"like-minded"* and practice and show *"the same love"* with which they were comforted with, through their union with Christ.

> *Philippians 2:1-2 (NIV) "1 Therefore if you have any encouragement from being united with Christ, if any comfort from his love, if any common sharing in the Spirit, if any tenderness and **compassion**, 2 then **make my joy complete by being like-minded, having the same love, being one in spirit and of one mind**."*

How do we apply this in our daily Lives?

We value our relationship and union with Christ by walking in His footsteps and desiring to live and be like Him. One of the ways in which we give credence to this union with Christ is by being compassionate.

- Take time to show *kind-heartedness* and care towards people around you on a daily basis.
- Take time to look for the *challenges* people face around you.

May the challenges people face, move us in the same way as Christ was **moved with compassion**. He was moved with such **deep compassion** that He reached out to **help us in our weaknesses**.

- Show *concern*, sympathy and *understanding* for the weaknesses people face daily.

One of the most powerful ways in which we can show our true compassion, like Christ, is to help people in their weaknesses.

- Take time to see how you can help and *assist* people wherever you find yourself.
- Take time to *listen* to people.

Helping and giving a **willing listening ear** to listen to the cries of people is sometimes **the biggest show of compassion** and **care** they need and require.

- Take time to *care* and be *kind*.

Caring

Compassionate Care is about *caring*, and **Caring is being thoughtful, sympathetic** and **lovingly helpful** towards others, especially **considering their cares, burdens and concerns.**

Jesus offers compassionate care when He says to the weary to come to Him.

> *Matthew 11:28 (NIV)* **"Come to me,** *all you who are weary and* **burdened,** *and* **I will give you rest."**

The Apostle Paul exhorts Believers to **"carry each other's burdens."** It is when we **take time to notice the burdens people bear,** and then **offer to help** them with the very things just encumber them, that we put into practice compassionate care.

> *Galatians 6:2 (NIV)* "2 **Carry each other's burdens,** *and in this way, you will fulfill the law of Christ."*

> *1 Peter 5:2-3 (NIV)* 2 **Be shepherds of God's flock** *that is* **under your care, watching over them**—*not because you must, but because you are willing, as* **God wants you to be;** *not pursuing dishonest gain, but* **eager to serve;** *3 not lording it over those entrusted to you, but* **being examples to the flock.**

Although this Scripture exhorts Leaders to practice care, by watching over those entrusted to their care, this also speaks to each one of us who desire to be fruitful in the Kingdom of God.

- Take care of your own *family*.

One way we provide compassionate care is by **caring for our own families**, our **parents** and **grandparents**. It pleases God when we take care of **widows** and **orphans**.

> *1 Timothy 5:4 (NIV)* *"4 But if a widow has children or grandchildren, these should learn first of all to* **put their religion into practice by caring for their own family** *and so repaying their parents and grandparents, for this is pleasing to God."*

> *James 1:27 (NIV)* *"27 Religion that God our Father accepts as pure and faultless is this:* **to look after orphans and widows in their distress** *and to keep oneself from being polluted by the world."*

Every time we **take care of the needs of others**, we have an opportunity to **practice compassionate care**.

- Jesus instructed Peter to: *"Take care of my sheep!"*

Of all the things Jesus could have addressed with Peter, when He restored him in Luke 21, after his denying of the Lord, He asked him to "**take care of my sheep.**"

> *John 21:16 (NIV)* *"16 Again Jesus said, 'Simon son of* **John, do you love me?'** *He answered, 'Yes, Lord, you know that I love you." Jesus said, "Take care of my sheep.""*

In one sense the Lord could just as well have asked us the same question today: "**Do you love me?**" He could also just as well be answering us: "**Good, then feed my sheep and take care of my sheep.**"

What does it mean to really care?

- Being caring is being mindful, *considerate* and helpful to others.
- Being Caring is to be lovingly *concerned* for the welfare of others.
- To be caring is to be *sensitive* to the needs and cares of others, and to treat them with compassion.

One of the characteristics Jesus desires His Disciples to have is to *"take care"* of His sheep.

To put it into the Words of Paul; to *"take care"* is to *put our religion into practice.*

Philippians 4:9 (NIV) 9 Whatever you have learned or received or heard from me, or seen in me—*put it into practice.* And the God of peace will be with you.

We do what we value. Well, one of those *true values* in the Kingdom of God is to *take care* of those around us, and under our care.

How do we put this into practice?

- Firstly, we *show care* when *we take note* of *the cares, concerns* and *burdens* of people around us, especially those entrusted to our care, and
- Secondly, we *take care* when *we do something about it*, by *showing love*, being *helpful* and *assisting.*
- To be caring is to *be mindful* and *considerate* in a way that shows those concerned that you really care.
- *We take care* when we *carry each other's burdens.*

One of the ways to care is to *relief the burden* for a *working single parent* by offering to look after their children to enable them to go and work, enabling them to earn a wage without having to add more pressure of having to *pay for childcare*. Another way is to *assist with providing temporary care* for people with *ageing parents*. *Every time we step up to meet the needs of others*, especially when we've taken the time to notice their distress and need of help, *we honour God* by providing care.

- *Take care* of each other, and *carry each other's burdens*, and in this way *fulfill the way of love*.

Afterword

I pray that we will all have open hearts and eyes to observe the cares and concerns with which people are burdened around us, and then to have the heart to step up into providing whatever we are able to give to make their burdens easier to bear.

6

WALKING WORTHILY

A s we grow in our Faith, and *our responsibility* and *accountability increase*, so does our *consciousness to walk worthily* according to the trust God placed in us. *As we increase in fruitfulness* and more *souls look to us* for *guidance, directions* and *an example to follow*, we need to *think,* and rethink, *how we speak, what we say and do*, and *what example* we are to others. We constantly *consider our ways, actions, whereabouts*, especially as to how they might advance the Kingdom of God.

We are Christ's Ambassadors!

We normally think of "*walk*" as it relates to how we *move from one place to another*. However, *there is another sense* in which this word is used. In the following two portions of Scripture we see that it refers to *a person's walk of life*. *What we do* with our life and *how we live our lives* can be *described as our walk*.

> *Ephesians 4:1-3 (NIV) "[1] As a prisoner for the Lord, then, I urge you to **live a life worthy** of the calling you have received. [2] Be completely humble and gentle; be patient, bearing with one*

another in love. [3] Make every effort to keep the unity of the Spirit through the bond of peace."

The Apostle Paul exhorts the Ephesian Believers to **live life** in *a worthy manner, according to the Calling* they received. This is to **display** such **high regard** for the calling, that one **quenches one's appetites** and **desires** to match the high regard with which one holds the Calling on one's life.

We are further exhorted to **live worthily out of gratitude** to be granted such a Calling and opportunity to serve the Master in the extension of His Kingdom. To even contemplate *"living worthily"* one has to live out of **gratitude** as well as live in such a way as to show *the regard* one has for *the calling.*

As an expression of this desire and willingness to give expression to *"live a life worthy of the calling,"* Paul exhorts them to show it by being *"completely humble, gentle, patient and loving."* Our *intentional efforts* to **keep unity** is another *way of expressing* our desire to live a life worthy of the calling we have received.

> *Ephesians 5:1-2 (NIV) "[1] Be imitators of God, therefore, as dearly loved children [2] and live a life of love, just as Christ loved us and gave himself up for us as a fragrant offering and sacrifice to God."*

In the book of Ephesians, Paul uses the word "*walk*" **6 times**. Each time he does, he uses it in the sense of *one's conduct* or *manner of living*. Paul writes to the Ephesian believers to show them how they are to live their lives as they pass through this world, since we are only journeying through as *pilgrims and strangers.* He is writing to teach them how they are to live their lives.

Defining "walk"

The **Strong's Greek** word "*Peripateo*" is translated as *"walk"* but strongly suggest hebraistically, *to live, to regulate one's life, and to*

<u>*conduct oneself*</u>.

It also suggests: *to walk, to behave*, to *conduct oneself, to lead a life*, be occupied, walk about, and walk around.[1] The Amplified Bible neatly expounds on this "*walk*" in Ephesians 5 verses 1 and 2.

> *Ephesians 5:1-2 (AMP) "[5:1] THEREFORE BE imitators of God [copy Him and follow His example], as well-beloved children [imitate their father]. [2] And **walk in love**, [esteeming and delighting in one another] as Christ loved us and gave Himself up for us, a slain offering and sacrifice to God [for you, so that it became] a sweet fragrance."*

From these two portions and versions *it is clear* that it is *God's desire* that we *walk worthily*, both *as examples* for others to follow, as well as *expressing our high regard* for the Calling with which He called each one of us.

Christ's Ambassadors

When *I think of an Ambassador*, I think of someone whose *conduct is stately*, holds *high moral ground*, and one who *acts appropriately* and *responsibly*. I think of an Ambassador as the *most trustworthy* and *reliable representative* a Country has to present its case, as well as *stand for its beliefs* in a *dignified* and *consistent way*. I think of someone who *is righteous, just* and *dignified*.

Now, when the Apostle Paul makes this *direct association* between *us and Ambassadors*, it is quite a *significant* thing. Just pause and think about it: *Ambassadors of Christ*.

> *2 Corinthians 5:20 (NIV) "20 **We are therefore Christ's ambassadors**, as though God were making his appeal through us. We implore you on Christ's behalf: Be reconciled to God."*

As an Ambassador, we both *represent Christ* and *His Kingdom*, as well as carry the representative task of *"imploring people on Christ's behalf"* to *be reconciled* to God.

This Ambassadorial Call and task requires of us to live worthily.

What does this mean for me? What should I do?

I believe that it *requires us* to *rethink* our *liberties, actions, responses, conduct, speech* and *attendances* in a more responsible way, as *everything we say and do reflects on Christ* and *His Kingdom*.

> *1 Corinthians 6:12 (NIV)* "*12 'I have the right to do anything,'* you *say—but not everything is beneficial. 'I have the right to do anything'—but I will not be mastered by anything.*"

On a few occasions we see this matter discussed by the various Apostles. Here we have the Apostle Paul clearly stating that *we can do whatever we want*, however, that *not everything* we have the right to do is *necessarily beneficial*, or as He states it in this next verse: "*constructive.*"

> *1 Corinthians 10:23 (NIV)* "*23 I have the right to do anything,'* you *say—but not everything is beneficial. 'I have the right to do anything'—but not everything is constructive. 24 No one should seek their own good, but the good of others.*"

In this address of the same principle the *emphasis falls on us to act* and *behave* for *the advantage of others.* As we continue to read in this chapter, Paul exhorts us to contemplate what we "*eat or drink*" or "*whatever we do,*" we should do all *for the Glory of God,* and as far as it is possible *not cause*, through our eating and drinking and whatever we do, *someone to stumble.* The purpose for living a worthy life is that none should perish, but all may be saved.

> *1 Corinthians 10:31-33 (NIV)* "*31 So whether you eat or drink or whatever you do, do it all for the glory of God. 32 Do not cause*

anyone to <u>stumble</u>, whether Jews, Greeks or the church of God
*— 33 even as I try to please everyone in every way. For **I am***
not seeking my own good** but the good of many, **so that they
***may be saved**."*

I know that I am labouring the point, however, I have seen, and **heard, the disappointments** and **expressed disillusionments** from **young Believers** who came out of the world and in earnest make strides to put into practice the Word of God, and then, to their dismay, observe the **compromised lives** some so called leaders live. I have equally heard the arguments from those who have **turned away from their faith** because of the **inconsistencies** and **indiscretions** they **observed** from **so-called leaders.**

Now, the questions I hear some of you are contemplating are:

- *"So, should I then not just rather step back until I overcome my fleshly struggles?"* or
- *"It is too hard, why even try to be a good example?"* or
- *"I don't know whether I am ready or willing to give up some of the things I enjoy for the sake of not offending someone?"*

I pray that the Holy Spirit will help you to allow *the **Will of God**,* and *His purpose* for your life, to be *fulfilled.* I grew up with a chorus that said: *"I want to live the way He wants me to live..."* This is still my song and prayer daily.

*Romans 14:19 (NIV) "19 **Let us therefore make every effort to do***
what leads to peace and to mutual edification. 20 Do not
***destroy the work of God for the sake of food.** All food is clean,*
but it is wrong for a person to eat anything that causes someone
*else to stumble. 21 **It is better not to eat meat or drink wine or***
to do anything else that will cause your brother or sister to
***fall.** 22 So, whatever you believe about these things keep*
between yourself and God. Blessed is the one who does not
condemn himself by what he approves."

For the sake of Christ and for the *sake of mutual edification*, let us *make every effort* to *not destroy the work of God* over *food* or what we *drink* or what we *do*, but rather *make earnest pursuits* to do those things that will *advance peace* and *mutual edification*.

> *Colossians 3:17 (NIV) "17 And whatever you do, whether in word or deed, do it all in the name of the Lord Jesus, giving thanks to God the Father through him."*

I think that this should kind of be a built-in barometer in each one of us to govern our actions by asking:

"Am I honouring God by what I am doing or saying now?"

May we *align our words and deeds* to live as *true Ambassadors* of the Kingdom of God.

Of course, there is a lot that can be said on this subject, however, let me share one more thought for our contemplation.

Our "walk" has a direct impact on our ability to reach people for Christ.

> *Colossians 4:5-6 (NIV) "5 Be wise in the way you act toward outsiders; make the most of every opportunity. 6 Let your conversation be always full of grace, seasoned with salt, so that you may know how to answer everyone."*

I often have meetings with people in cafés and restaurants, and I am always mindful that others might hear and listen to our conversation. I therefor keep this Scripture in the forefront of my heart, to remind me, to keep my conversation filled with grace, compassion and understanding. I pray that you too will make the most of every opportunity to live worthily.

Action Steps

In conclusion of our time together, can we pause for a moment and consider each of the following areas in our lives, especially as it directly impacts others. We are clearly called upon to communicate the love and life of Christ to others through each of these areas.

- Consider whether your activities, engagements, or example, advance or hinder how others see Christ.
- Consider whether there are areas that you need to make adjustments.
- Consider ways in which you could be more Ambassadorial.

1. **Words.** (Consider the words you are using that are inappropriate , slanderous, demeaning, vulgar, or untruthful, if any. Consider how intentionally wholesome and upbuilding your words are.)

- Commit to cease the use these, and other swearwords or expletives to express yourself.
- Commit yourself to wholesome speech.

Name three areas where you can be more attentive or diligent in your speech.

_____

_____

_____

2. **Deeds.** (Consider your actions and reactions, that might be inconsiderate, inappropriate, demeaning, and inconsistent with that of being an example for others to follow.)

- I commit to careful observe my deeds, that they may always, in every circumstance and situation, honor God and encourage others to a deeper and more meaningful walk with God.

- I commit to be a living Testament.
- I commit my ways to God.

Name three specific areas where you commit yourself to apply this more astutely.

_____
_____
_____

3. Attendances. (Take a moment and consider places you go, or attend, that might cause weak people to stumble in their faith, if they see you there, or see you participating in those activities. We are in the world, not of the world.)

- I commit to withdraw my attendance from places, activities and gatherings that might bring disrepute to Christ and His Church, other than actively sharing my faith in those places.
- I commit to being more attentive, with who, and to where I spend my recreational time, as I understand that as an Ambassador I represent Christ and His Church.

Name at least one area where you commit to being more attentive, and why.

_____
_____
_____

4. Eating and drinking. (Take a moment and think about the various places where you frequently dine or simply have something to drink. Are there things that you eat or drink in these places, where others might see you, that might offend some who are weak in their faith? If the considered answer is "YES," then you might want to attend to not destroying the work of God because of what you eat or drink.)

If any, name the things which you intentionally will avoid and eliminate so as to not cause anyone to stumble or fall in their faith?

_____

_____

_____

5. Conversation of my life. (Think about the Open Letter you are out there in the world, on the streets and in the workplace.)

- Is your life a good communicator of the faith you profess?
- Is your faith visible to others to see?
- Do you have a positive and upbuilding effect on people around you?

What do you hope others see and report of your "Conversation"?

_____

_____

_____

6. What is that **ONE THING** that you will take with you from this session, that will change how people see you represent Christ in the future, and ultimately will see you being fruitful?

_____

_____

_____

_____

_____

7

WALKING IN THE SPIRIT

During this phase of Discipleship we learn the value and impact it has when we keep *a consistent walk* under the direction and guidance of the Holy Spirit. We keep this walk with the Holy Spirit since He is our Helper and the most powerful partner in our ministry.

> Galatians 5:16 (NIV) "16 So I say, **walk by the Spirit, and you will not gratify the desires of the flesh.** 17 For the flesh desires what is contrary to the **Spirit**, and the Spirit what is contrary to the flesh. **They are in conflict with each other**, so that you are not to do whatever you want. 18 But if you are led by the Spirit, you are not under the law."

> Galatians 5:25 (NIV) "25 Since we live by the Spirit, **let us keep in step with the Spirit.**"

The **Holy Spirit is** the most **tangible** and **sustainable Gift** we could ever receive from God. Having Him **live inside of us** gives us an enduring appreciation for His Presence and Power.

Led by the Spirit of the Lord

We all desire to be led by the Spirit of the Lord on a *daily basis*. Romans chapter 8 defines such a walk in the Spirit.

> *Romans 8:1 (NIV) "[8:1] There is therefore now **no condemnation** to them which are in Christ Jesus, **who walk not after the flesh, but after the Spirit.**"*

Walking in the Spirit positions us to a secure and affirming place without condemnation. A life of **walking in the Spirit** is **reserved for** those who have their **minds set** on what the **Holy Spirit desires**. The Bible teaches that if you truly desire life and peace, then allowing your mind to be controlled by the Holy Spirit will bring you to such a life.

> *Romans 8:5-6 (NIV) [5] Those who live according to the sinful nature have their minds set on what that nature desires; but **those who live in accordance with the Spirit have their minds set on what the Spirit desires.** [6] The mind of sinful man is death, but **the mind controlled by the Spirit is life and peace.** "*

When the Holy Spirit is in control of our lives then our sinful nature will not have such control over our lives. Yielding to the control of the Holy Spirit safeguards us from many unwanted acts and behaviours. By choosing to walk in the Spirit, we choose to walk in safety.

The **Holy Spirit's** presence also gives us that enduring *affirmation* that *we belong to God*. Remaining under the control and leading of the *Holy Spirit affirms* within us that *we are the sons of God*.

> *Romans 8:9 (NIV) "[9] You, however, are controlled not by the sinful nature but by the Spirit, **if the Spirit of God lives in you. And if anyone does not have the Spirit of Christ, he does not belong to Christ.**"*

Romans 8:13-14 (NIV) "[13] For if you live according to the sinful nature, you will die; but if by the Spirit you put to death the misdeeds of the body, you will live, [14] **because those who are led by the Spirit of God are sons of God.** *[15] For you did not receive a spirit that makes you a slave again to fear, but you received the Spirit of Sonship. And by him we cry,* **"Abba, Father."** *[16]* **The Spirit himself testifies with our spirit that we are God's children.**

Walking in **the Spirit ensures** that we live with a **source of quickening power inside** of us. The more you walk in the Spirit, the more you experience His quickening power released in your earthly body.

Romans 8:11 (NIV) "[11] And **if the Spirit** *of him who raised Jesus from the dead is* **living in you,** *he who raised Christ from the dead* **will also give life to your mortal bodies through his Spirit, who lives in you."**

Galatians 4:6 (NIV) "[6] **Because you are sons, God sent the Spirit of his Son into our hearts,** *the Spirit who calls out,* **"Abba, Father."**

The distinctive of Men of God, throughout the Word, was their submission to living under the control of the Spirit of God.

The presence of the Person of the **Holy Spirit** is that one **thread throughout the Bible** that confirms the defining **power that existed** in these men and woman. It was the Holy Spirit's Presence on the Judges that brought them into leading Israel into victory.

Judges 3:10-11 (NIV) "[10] **The Spirit of the LORD came upon him,** *so that he became Israel's judge * and went to war.* **The LORD gave** *Cushan-Rishathaim king of Aram* **into the hands of Othniel, who overpowered him.** *[11]* **So the land had peace for forty years,** *until Othniel son of Kenaz died."*

The Holy Spirit came *upon the smallest*, the *least* and the *most insignificant* young man and *made him* into one of the *most significant leaders* and *deliverers* Israel ever saw.

> *Judges 6:34 (NIV)* "*[34]* *Then the Spirit of the LORD came upon Gideon*, *and he blew a trumpet, summoning the Abiezrites to follow him.*"

The Spirit of the Lord came upon *Jephthah*. He led Israel into many victories.

> *Judges 11:29 (NIV)* *[29]* *Then the Spirit of the LORD came upon Jephthah*. *He crossed Gilead and Manasseh, passed through Mizpah of Gilead, and from there he advanced against the Ammonites.*

Judges chapter 14 and 15 tells us of how *Samson* became when the Spirit of the Lord came upon him.

> *Judges 14:6, 19 (NIV)* "*[6]* *The Spirit of the LORD came upon him in power so that he tore the lion apart with his bare hands* as he might have torn a young goat. But he told neither his father nor his mother what he had done. *[19]* *Then the Spirit of the LORD came upon him in power*. *He went down to Ashkelon, struck down thirty of their men, stripped them of their belongings and gave their clothes to those who had explained the riddle. Burning with anger, he went up to his father's house.*"

> *Judges 15:14 (NIV)* "*[14]* *As he approached Lehi, the Philistines came toward him shouting. The Spirit of the LORD came upon him in power. The ropes on his arms became like charred flax, and the bindings dropped from his hands.*"

When God called *Saul*, it was because of the Holy Spirit's presence that came on him that He knew God anointed him to be king.

> *1 Samuel 10:6-7 [6]* **The Spirit of the LORD will come upon you in power**, *and you will prophesy with them; and* **you will be changed into a different person.** *[7] Once these signs are fulfilled, do whatever your hand finds to do, for* **God is with you.**

Saul knew that God was with him because he became *fully aware* of the *presence of the Holy Spirit*. The same happened to *David* when *Samuel anointed him* to become Israel's second king. *David became aware* that the Spirit of the Lord came upon him in power.

> *1 Samuel 16:13-14 (NIV) "[13] So* **Samuel took the horn of oil and anointed him** *in the presence of his brothers, and* **from that day on the Spirit of the LORD came upon David in power.** *Samuel then went to Ramah."*

David frequently *credited the Holy Spirit* for *speaking* to him and *through him*. When he committed adultery with *Bathsheba*, beyond *begging for forgiveness*, he *pleaded with God* to *not take His Spirit away* from him. *David valued* the *presence of the Holy Spirit* upon his life.

> *2 Samuel 23:2 (NIV) "[2]* **"The Spirit of the LORD spoke through me;** *his word was on my tongue."*

The old Testament *prophets spoke* and wrote *as the Holy Spirit led* them. The Apostle *Peter* reiterates the presence and leading of the Holy Spirit when he *reminds us* of the *origin* and *reliability of the prophecies*.

> *2 Peter 1:21 (NIV) "21 For prophecy never had its origin in the human will, but prophets, though human,* **spoke from God as they were carried along by the Holy Spirit."**

It was during one of these times when the prophet *Isaiah* was *carried away by the Spirit* that *he wrote* about the manifold parts of the Holy Spirit.

> *Isaiah 11:2-3 (NIV)* "[2] *The Spirit of the LORD will rest on him—
> the Spirit of wisdom and of understanding, the Spirit of
> counsel and of power, the Spirit of knowledge and of the fear
> of the LORD— [3] and he will delight in the fear of the LORD.
> He will not judge by what he sees with his eyes, or decide by
> what he hears with his ears;"*

Clear messages came to the Prophets *by the Holy Spirit*. They walked in the Spirit and was aware when the Spirit of the Lord came upon them. *Ezekiel*, as many of the prophets, *heard the voice* of the *Holy Spirit* and then delivered the messages God gave them to give.

> *Ezekiel 11:5 (NIV)* "[5] Then *the Spirit of the LORD came upon me,
> and he told me to say: 'This is what the LORD says: That is
> what you are saying, O house of Israel, but I know what is
> going through your mind.'"*

The *Spirit of the Lord* was so *visibly strong on their lives* that even those who did not serve the Lord *recognised* His presence on His Servants' lives. *King Nebuchadnezzar recognised* the *Holy Spirit in Daniel.*

> *Daniel 4:18 (NIV)* "[18] 'This is the dream that I, King
> Nebuchadnezzar, had. Now, Belteshazzar, tell me what it
> means, for none of the wise men in my kingdom can interpret it
> for me. But you can, because the spirit of the holy gods is in
> you.'"*

Jesus recognised and *acknowledged the Holy Spirit upon his life* when he read from the scroll in the Synagogue. He stated that: "*the Spirit of the Lord is upon me.*"

> *Luke 4:18-19 (NIV)* "*[18]* '*The Spirit of the Lord is on me, because*
> *he has anointed me to preach good news to the poor. He has*
> *sent me to proclaim freedom for the prisoners and recovery of*
> *sight for the blind, to release the oppressed, [19] to proclaim the*
> *year of the Lord's favour.*'"

Philip was such a New Testament Believer who **walked in the**
Spirit, and was led by the Holy Spirit. One day the **Holy Spirit told him**
to **go** to **a certain chariot. He did** whatever **the Holy Spirit told him** and
the **result was** that **an Ethiopian Eunuch got saved** and was **baptised.**

> *Acts 4:29 (NIV)* "*[29]* The Spirit told Philip, "**Go to that chariot and**
> **stay near it.**""

It was their **willing yielding** to **the leading of the Holy Spirit** that **led**
to Barnabas and Paul being **commissioned** for their **apostolic journeys.**

> *Acts 13:2 (NIV)* "*[2]* While they were worshiping the Lord and
> fasting, **the Holy Spirit said,** "Set apart for me **Barnabas and**
> **Saul** for **the work** to which I have called them.""

Greater things come from the Spirit of God's empowerment.

The more we walk in the Spirit, **intentionally submitting ourselves** to His
leading, **the more** we will **experience His Power** made manifest in ways
not seen or heard of before.

> *Zechariah 4:6 (NIV)* "*[6]* So he said to me, "This is the word of the
> LORD to Zerubbabel: 'Not by might nor by power, but by my
> Spirit,' says the LORD Almighty."

Without His work in our lives, **no sanctification** can take place.
Without His work in our ministry we will see **no fruit** on our labours.
He changes hearts. He **Heals, delivers** and **convicts.** Walking in fellow-

ship with the Holy Spirit has many providential *advantages* since He is our *ultimate Teacher*. It is *His Anointing* on our lives that *makes* all the *difference*. Develop and *grow in* your *appreciation of the Holy Spirit*. Make it your ambition to *walk in a deep relationship* with him every day.

Action Steps

Awareness is one of the key aspects to develop, when we desire a constant walk in the Power of the Holy Spirit.

1. Know the Voice of the Holy Spirit

One of the areas we need to develop, is our awareness to the voice of the Holy Spirit. Sometimes the Holy Spirit speaks audibly loud and clear, but mostly He will speak to us in a still gentle voice. The more we develop an awareness and sensitivity to hearing His voice, the more we will notice it and respond to it. Grow in your awareness to know His voice in your life, not just during worship services, although that is sometimes one place where we are more in tune to hear His voice but try and develop an awareness of His voice during normal life circumstances. Take a few moments to listen to the voice of the Holy Spirit. Jesus once said: "My sheep know my voice and they listen." *Be that sheep who know His voice* and listen.

Do you know the voice of the Holy Spirit in your life? _____

How does the Holy Spirit speak to you? _____

_____

What can you do to hear Him better? _____

_____

_____

2. Messages.

Develop an expectation and awareness to receive messages from God, first to yourself, but then also messages for others. I believe God wants to speak, guide and encourage His people every day. We, therefore, have an opportunity, and a responsibility, to listen for those messages from God. They might come when God speak to us by the Holy Spirit's voice inside of us, or they might come through other Messengers who bring a Word to us, or they might come through our time in the Word. There are many ways in which God can bring messages to us. Our intentional focus requires that we listen and look out for those messages from God. I am constantly reminded of the words Jesus quoted from the Book of Deuteronomy chapter eight.

> Deuteronomy 8:3 (NIV) 3 He humbled you, causing you to hunger and then feeding you with manna, which neither you nor your ancestors had known, to teach you that man does not live on bread alone but on every word that comes from the mouth of the LORD.

We live on the messages He give us daily, whether that be words to guide us, direct us, teach us, discipline us, or words that He desires us to deliver to others.

Have you ever received a message from God? _____

How frequently do you receive messages from God? _____

Do you receive messages from God for others? _____

Do you deliver these messages from God to others? _____

What is your desire related to the receiving and delivering of messages? _____

_____

_____

3. Missions.

God saved us for a purpose. His purposes become our mission assignments. The Great Commission is encased with the ensuing word "GO." In fact, nothing happens without us going. It is only once we "GO" and preach that people can come to salvation. It is only then that we will have new Believers to Baptise. It is only then that we will have Young Believers to teach. It is only then that we will see and experience the promise of "*signs following*" and "*the Lord working with*" us.

Have you ever been given an assignment by God? _____

What did the Lord send you to do? _____

You have a sense that God has a greater mission purpose for your life? If yes, what is that Mission purpose? _____

_____

_____

Do you at times sense that God's Mission purpose for others is revealed to you? _____

_____

4. Activating some Gift or Grace.

Another area where we observe and develop our continual walk in the Holy Spirit is by personally eagerly desiring and developing the Gifts of the Holy Spirit in our lives. We also grow and develop in activating the same in those around us as well. Paul practiced this with those Believers in the church in Rome.

> Romans 1:11-12 (NIV) 11 I long to see you so that I may impart to you some spiritual gift to make you strong— 12 that is, that you and I may be mutually encouraged by each other's faith.

The elders also practiced this when they laid hands on Timothy.

> 1 Timothy 4:14 (NIV) 14 Do not neglect your gift, which was given you through prophecy when the body of elders laid their hands on you.

Which Gifts are you actively pursuing and engaging presently? __

_____

_____

Have you ever sensed that you knew the Gift of God on another Believer's life? _____

Have you told them what you sensed God show you? _____

How often do you lay hands on other Believers to impart some spiritual Gift? _____

Do you have a desire to be used by God in this matter more? ____

5. Power and Presence of the Holy Spirit.

Recognizing the Power of the Holy Spirit in one's life is *essential* to a *prolonged and enduring walk* in the power of the Holy Spirit. On the one hand *an awareness* and *recognition* of the *Power of the Holy Spirit protects us* from thinking that it is our *super-human abilities* that allows us to *sustainably function at a high pace,* and simultaneously be so *spiritually alert* and able to *minister for hours* in *varying circumstances* and *situations.* On the other hand, this recognition and awareness *maintains our reliance* and *dependency* on *His Mighty Power.*

> Acts 1:8 (NIV) 8 But you will receive power when the Holy
> Spirit comes on you; and you will be my witnesses in
> Jerusalem, and in all Judea and Samaria, and to the ends
> of the earth."

Jesus promised that we *"will receive Power when the Holy Spirit"* come upon us. The more people recognise and walk in the Power of the Holy Spirit, the more we see them *boldly seize every opportunity* to *bear witness* of their unrelenting faith in Jesus.

We are *able to minister days on end, hour after hour,* because of His Mighty Power of the Holy Spirit. The Power of the Holy Spirit allows us to maintain a sustained spiritual alertness to minister in the Holy Spirit to those in front of us. This was the experience in the Life of Jesus, His Disciples, and those who through the years kept a close walk in the Presence and Power of the Holy Spirit.

> Luke 5:17 (NIV) 17 One day Jesus was teaching, and Pharisees
> and teachers of the law were sitting there. They had come
> from every village of Galilee and from Judea and
> Jerusalem. And *the power of the Lord was with Jesus to heal
> the sick.*

Jesus recognized the Power of the Holy Spirit to Heal people. The result was that many received their healing that day.

Luke 6:19 (NIV) 19 and the people all tried to touch him,
because power was coming from him and healing
them all.

The Power of the Holy Spirit was so strong on Jesus that people received their healing by simply touching Him. The Apostles also experienced this Power of the Holy Spirit on their lives.

Acts 4:33 (NIV) 33 With great power the apostles continued to
testify to the resurrection of the Lord Jesus. And God's
grace was so powerfully at work in them all

One moment we minister healing, then next we cast out devils, the next we operate with the Gift of Faith or Working of Miracles, then next we minister a Word of Wisdom or Word of Knowledge, and then in between we keep a group of people focused on His Presence and Power in operation. This is only possible through our subordinate flow with the Holy Spirit.

Have you ever sensed the Power of the Holy Spirit in your life? ___

How often are you aware of His Power on your life? _____

What helps you most in attracting the Power and Presence of the Holy Spirit in your life? _____

_____

_____

What have you become aware of when the Power of the Holy Spirit came on you? _____

_____

_____

Have you become aware of various workings of the Holy Spirit when you minister? _____

_____

_____

What difference will the Power of the Holy Spirit make in your life and Ministry? _____

_____

6. Work of the Holy Spirit.

The Holy Spirit is amazing and recognising His work wherever we are will most certainly enable us to have a more fulfilled and wholesome experience of His Presence and immense Power.

- Sometimes He desires to *commission people for service* such as was the case in the church in Antioch when the Holy Spirit spoke and set Barnabas and Paul aside for the work to which they were called.
- Sometimes the Holy Spirit wants to bring *healing and restore* people *spiritually, emotionally, relationally, physically* or on a National basis. Unless we are attentive to what work the Holy Spirit does in a place, we might miss to cooperate with Him.
- Sometimes the *conviction of the Holy Spirit* is strong in a place and many salvations will take place if we tune in and flow with Him.
- Sometimes the Holy Spirit's *sanctifying work* is strong in a gathering. By declaring the overwhelming purpose of the Presence of the Lord in a place many times activates and releases that operation to accomplish tremendous things in people's lives.

To enjoy a sustained walk in the Spirit we are required to develop an awareness in all of these areas.

Have you ever sensed what they Holy Spirit wanted to do in a gathering of Believers? _____

What did you become aware of? _____

_____

How do you think you can become more aware of what the Holy Spirit wants to do around you? _____

_____

Do you think there is a connection between the areas in which you are comfortable to minister, and the areas which you might sense in which the Holy Spirit wants to minister? _____

8

PRACTICING HOSPITALITY

One of the requirements for an Elder is that he or she needs to *be hospitable.*

Romans 12:13 (NIV) "13 Share with the Lord's people who are in need. Practice hospitality."

This instruction from Paul to the Romans was not a suggestion, but a definitive instruction. *Practice Hospitality!*

How do you practice hospitality?

- We practice hospitality *by inviting people to our house.* You can't start practicing without people.
- Choose a day where you are more relaxed like on a Saturday afternoon or Sunday afternoon.
- Start by inviting people over *in between mealtimes* for coffee or tea, and at most maybe some cookies. This could be extended to having *two,* or even *more couples over at a time.*
- Take this time to *practice* your *"deepening relationship*

questions" which you explored during the **Shepherd Leader Course.**

- Inviting people over for dinner is best done with those with whom you find affinity. It is much easier to visit with people who are easy to hold a conversation with.
- *Evening visits* are great, but if you are new to this, be aware that these kind of invites often lean towards being an **unspoken invitation for dinner.**

There might be an **unspoken expectation** that **you invited them for dinner**, if your invitation is for **a time during** which people **in your culture** regularly **have dinner** at home. This is especially true if you invite people over for an evening visit, especially if the invitation is over a weekend.

Think through the idea before you invite people. If you are not comfortable to hosting people, then this might be better left until you are more comfortable to practice hospitality over a dinner appointment. This is the easier kind of practicing hospitality.

Hosting Angels

> *Hebrews 13:2 (NIV) 2 Do not forget to show hospitality to strangers, for by so doing some people have shown hospitality to angels without knowing it.*

This kind of hospitality is of course much more stretching to the average Believer, especially for those from more developed nations. This hosting of strangers comes as a major stretch to most; however, this is exactly what the Lord calls us to be open to, to practice. To host Angels comes with an openness to hosting strangers first.

This kind of hospitality requires that we actually host strangers.

The more involved we get with people and practicing hospitality, the more we might, unexpectedly, be called upon to show hospitality. This Scripture is quite an amazing Scripture because it opens up the very real possibility to us hosting Angels.

Wouldn't you love to host an Angel in your house?

The only way to enjoy the privilege of hosting an angel is by being open to showing hospitality to strangers, even when that might not come at a convenient time. The Apostle Peter is quite upfront about this required discipline for Believers to practice.

> *1 Peter 4:9 (NIV) 9 Offer hospitality to one another without grumbling.*

We are encouraged to show hospitality to one another, without grumbling.

Who is this "One Another?"

This *"one another"* starts with *fellow Believers*. Showing hospitality is possibly one of *the greatest signs* that *you don't just live for yourself*, a selfish, self-centred life, but one *for the advantage* and *encouragement of others*. I love the way the Amplified Bible expounds on it.

> *1 Peter 4:9 (AMPC) "9 **Practice hospitality to one another,** (especially to those of the household of faith.) [Be hospitable, be a lover of strangers, with brotherly affection for the unknown guests, the foreigners, the poor, and all others who come your way who are of Christ's body.] And [in each instance] do it ungrudgingly (cordially and graciously, without complaining but as representing Him)."*

A few things stand out for me here:

- **First**, the "*one another*" stands to primarily mean "*the household of faith*" fellow Believers.

- **Secondly**, the extension to include "*strangers, unknown guests, foreigners, the poor*, and all others who come your way" show the extent of how open we need to be to showing hospitality.

I don't know about you, but just talking about it, and exploring it together, makes me anxious, but that is exactly what God is asking of us.

- **Thirdly**, this Scripture exhorts us to practice this open hospitality "*ungrudgingly*." That is: *without complaining, moaning and groaning*.

We ought to be open to extend hospitality to all of these strangers, *without complaining*, but "*cordially and graciously*," as true representatives of Christ, and as if we are hosting Him, ourselves.

I can't but think of the one message *Christ* brought once, when He **commended His righteous** for *hosting, feeding, and clothing Him*. We read about this full description of showing hospitality in Matthew chapter 25.

> *Matthew 25:35-36 (NIV) 35 For I was hungry and you gave me something to eat, I was thirsty and you gave me something to drink, I was a stranger and you invited me in, 36 I needed clothes and you clothed me, I was sick and you looked after me, I was in prison and you came to visit me.'*

They were amazed at Him commending them for things they did not even think they did. They immediately interrupted Him by asking as to when they actually did these noble tasks. The Bible tells us of their amazement and questioning of the Lord:

> *Matthew 25:37-39 (NIV) 37 "Then the righteous will answer him,* **'Lord, when did we see you hungry and feed you, or thirsty and give you something to drink?** *38 When did we see you a stranger and invite you in, or needing clothes and clothe you? 39 When did we see you sick or in prison and go to visit you?'*

The Lord's response should further inspire us to step up in our practicing of hospitality. He responded to their amazement by saying:

> *Matthew 25:40 (NIV) 40 "The King will reply,* 'Truly *I tell you,* **whatever you did for one of the least of these** *brothers and sisters of mine,* **you did for me.'**

Hospitality is in a sense defined within these few scriptures:

- *Feed the hungry*
- *Quench the thirst* of those who need something to drink
- *Provide a place to sleep* for those in need of a place to stay
- *Clothe those needing clothes*
- *Visit* the *sick* and *those in prison*

Our practice of hospitality towards "***the least of these***" is as good as practicing hospitality to Jesus Himself. It is well noticed and appreciated by Jesus, it is no wonder that one of the requirements of Leadership in the local church is that of "***hospitality.***"

The Apostle Paul taught this principle to his spiritual son, Timothy.

> *1 Timothy 3:2 (NIV) "2 Now* **the overseer is to be** *above reproach, faithful to his wife, temperate, self-controlled, respectable,* **hospitable,** *able to teach,"*

What are some other practical ways in which we could be more hospitable?

- We could be *more hospitable* by having *a clean house* that is *always open* to those who need to come over *for a chat, prayer* or some *ministry*.
- Keeping your *house clean* and *presentable* is always *a good indication* of *one's diligence in keeping good disciplines*.
- Offering a *glass of water* on *arrival* always makes a huge *impression* of your *hospitality*.
- You *don't need* to necessarily *cook every time* people come over, but a simple *glass of water* when they arrive goes a long way in presenting yourself as *a good host*.

Matthew 10:42 (NIV) 42 And if anyone gives even a cup of cold water to one of these little ones who is my disciple, truly I tell you, that person will certainly not lose their reward."

- **Cleanliness and hospitality are two key essentials to practice for every aspiring Christian Leader.**

I always remember what my Dad taught me, that:

Next to Godliness is Cleanliness!

He always made the *connection* between the way *people's shoes are kept*, and *their walk with God*. He said that: *"If they make no time to clean their shoes, they possibly make no time for keeping a clean and devoted life either."*

So, *clean shoes*, clean and *neatly ironed clothes*, a *clean house, clean dishes*, a *clean yard, well-kept flowerbeds, clean offices* and *studies*, are all *good indicators* of *one's preparedness* to *host people*, and of the cleanliness with which we keep our lives.

You might be *willing to host people*, but *they might decline* the offer when they know that they *might* have to *fend with filth, unkept animals* and an *unruly house.* In their minds, even the local Park bench might be a cleaner and more secure option. Let this not be true in your and my life, *may we practice cleanliness* next to *godliness.*

A final *suggestion* to being *a great host* regards *prayer.*

- Always offer prayer before your guests leave your house.

Pray the Aaronic Blessing over them, at least, but mostly *pray* that *the Lord will go with them. Bless them* in all their ways. *Bless their family,* their *work,* their *finances,* their *labour for the Lord. Pray* for God's *protection* over them, and *His provision* for them. *I often* also take time to *pray some Psalm,* like *Psalm 23* over them. *May they leave* with *the Blessing of God* over their lives.

May *their association* with *visiting you* always be kept with *thoughts of* your *spiritual ministry to them* and "*that prayer*" that *you prayed.* Be a blessing!

Food is great, if it is within your means to provide any, *but* this is *not the standard* that will *qualify or disqualify you* for being *a great host. Having great fellowship* and having a *great visit are wonderful,* but the thing that I believe *God really wants* is that we *make a spiritual deposit in their lives* that will be *long remembered beyond* the *food* and *fellowship.*

Conclusion

This Step will *really help* you into *becoming* a *World class Leader,* fit and prepared to lead from the front. It is an exciting journey, and during this phase you'll see how your *Disciples become* true *spiritual sons and daughters* who *come of age* and desire to learn to *carry the values and principles* on to the *next generation.* It is *only when* your *Disciples start putting things into practice* that you will *find this step* of *immense value.*

Assimilation Action Steps

1. Practice Hospitality!

How do we practice hospitality? *By inviting people to our house. By inviting people for coffee or tea. By inviting people for meals. By practicing our use of "deepening relationship" questions.*

2. The timing of evening invitations need to be considered. Why? *Evening invitations could be seen as unspoken invitations for dinner.*

3. Hosting Angels. When are we most likely to host Angels? *Only when we open our homes to extend hospitality to strangers.*

4. 1 Peter chapter 4 verse 9 advices that we offer hospitality without, doing what? *Grumbling.*

5. What is another principle that we learn about ourselves through this verse? *We learn that we stopped living just for ourselves, but for the advantage and benefit of others.*

6. Who does the "One Another" primarily refer to in this verse? *The Household of Believers.*

7. In the Amplified Bible Version we learn that our Hospitality need also to be extended to others. Who are those others? *The others refer to strangers, unknown guests, foreigners, the poor, and those who cross paths with you.*

8. Jesus encapsulate the extend of hospitality through His message in Matthew 25 verses 35 to 40. Name at least three things the righteous did for which they were commended. *They were commended for feeding Him, giving Him something to drink, clothing Him, inviting Him in even though He was a stranger to them, visiting Him while He was sick, and visiting Him in prison.*

9. What is the simplest thing we can offer people to show them hospitality? *We can offer them a glass of water.*

10. Complete the sentence. *Next to godliness is cleanliness!*

11. Which areas are of particular concern for us to keep clean to be able to practice good hospitality? *Our house, dishes, garden, clothes, study's, and shoes.*

12. What is a good practice to have, before visitors leave your home. *Pray blessing over your guests before they leave your house.*

9

OTHER BOOKS BY DR HENDRIK J VORSTER

Discipleship Foundations - Step One - Salvation Disciple Manual

Step One - Salvation

This Course explores the "How to" be Born Again and to establish a solid Foundation for your faith in Jesus Christ. It is based on Hebrews chapter 6 verses 1 and 2, and explores:

Repentance of dead works,
Faith in God,
Baptisms,
Laying on of hands,
Resurrection of the dead, and
Eternal Judgement

Teacher Manuals and Video Teaching material are available through our website: www.churchplantinginstitute.com

Discipleship Foundations Step Two - Values and Spiritual Disciplines Disciple Manual

Step Two - Values and Spiritual Disciplines Disciple Manual

This Course explores the "How to" develop spiritual disciplines as well as 52 Values Jesus taught. It is based on the teachings of Jesus to His Disciples, and explores:

Spiritual Disciplines

The disciplines we explore are: Reading, meditating on the Word of God, Prayer, Stewardship, Fasting, Servanthood, Simplicity, Worship, and Witnessing.

Values of the Kingdom of God

Humility, Mournfulness, meekness, Spiritual Passion, Mercifulness, Purity, Peacemaker, Patient endurance, Example, Custodian, Reconciliatory, Resoluteness, Loving, Discreetness, Forgiving, Kingdom of God Investor, God-minded, Kingdom of God prioritiser, Introspective, Persistent, Considerate, Conservative, Fruit-bearing, Practitioner, Accountability, Faithful, Childlikeness, Unity, Servanthood, Loyalty, Gratefulness, Stewardship, Obedience, Carefulness, Compassion, Caring, Confidence, Steadfastness, Contentment, Teachable, Deference, Diligence, Trustworthiness, Gentleness, Discernment, Truthfulness, Generous, Kindness, Watchfulness, Perseverance, Honouring and Submissive.

Teacher Manuals and Video Teaching material are available through our website: www.churchplantinginstitute.com

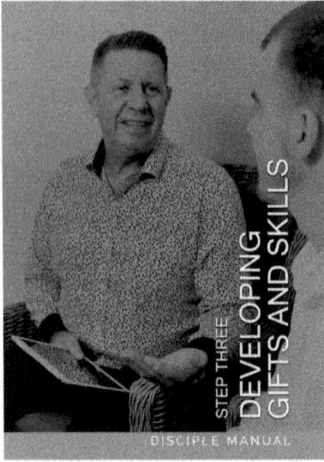

Discipleship Foundations Step Three - Developing Gifts and Skills

Step Three - Developing Gifts and Skills

This course is run through five weekend encounters. These weekend encounters have been designed to help Disciples discover their spiritual gifts, as well as learn skills to use their gifts, and to serve the Lord for the extension of His Kingdom. The Weekend Encounters are:

Gifts Discovery Weekend Encounter

We learn about Ministerial Office gifts, Service gifts, and Supernatural Spiritual Gifts. We discover our own, and then learn How we may use them to build up the local Church.

Survey of the Bible Weekend Encounter

During this weekend we do a survey of the Bible, from Genesis to Revelation. We also learn about the History of the Bible as well as How we can make most of our time in the Word.

Sharing your Faith Weekend Encounter

During this weekend we learn about the Gospel message, and How to share our faith effectively.

Overcoming Weekend Encounter

During this weekend we deal with those thistles and thorns that smother the growth and harvest of the good seed sown into our lives. We address How to overcome fear, unforgiveness, lust and the cares of the world with faith and obedience.

Shepherd Leader Weekend Encounter

During this weekend encounter we learn about being a Good Shepherd, and How to best disciple in a small group.

Teacher Manuals and Video Teaching material are available from our website: www.churchplantinginstitute.com

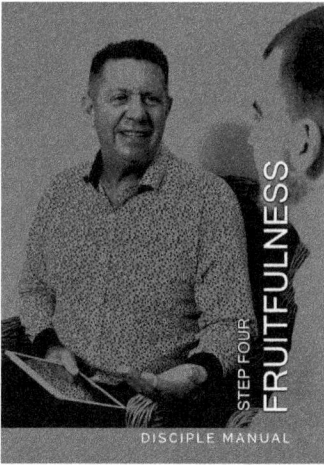

Discipleship Foundations Step Four - Fruitfulness

Step Four - Discipling Fruit-Producers

We were saved to serve. This course has been designed to mobilise Believers, from Learners to Practitioners. These sessions have been prepared for individual use, with those who are bearing fruit, and want to produce more fruit. Developing these areas in a sustained and systematic manner will ensure both fruitfulness and multiplication. Attending to these areas will ensure that you bear lasting fruit.

We explore:

1. Introduction.
2. Walking with purpose.
3. Build purposeful relationships. Finding Worthy Men
4. Priesthood. Praying effectively for those entrusted to you.
5. Caring compassionately.
6. Walking worthily.
7. Walking in the Spirit.
8. Practicing hospitality.

Teacher Manuals and Video Teaching material are available from our COURSES link from our website at:

www.churchplantinginstitute.com

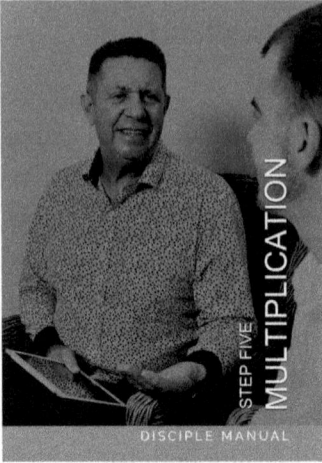

Step Five - Multiplication

This course was designed to assist fruit-producing disciples to live a life that will encourage a lifetime of fruitfulness. It will also give our disciples skills and guidelines to navigate their disciples through seasons of challenge and growth. This course is packed with Leadership advancing principles. The more these areas are addressed and encouraged, the more we will experience growth and multiplication. We explore:

1. Vision and dreams.
2. Set Godly Goals.
3. Character development
4. Gifts development - Impartation and Activation
5. Fruitfulness comes through constant challenge.
6. Relationships - Family, Children and Friends
7. The Power of encouragement
8. Finances - Personal and Ministry finances
9. Dealing with setbacks

- How to deal with failure?
- How to deal with betrayal?
- How to deal with rejection?
- How to deal with trials?
- How to deal with despondency?

10. Eternal rewards

Teacher Manuals and Video Teaching material are available from our website: www.churchplantinginstitute.com

VALUES
OF THE
KINGDOM
OF
GOD

Dr. Hendrik J. Vorster

Values of the Kingdom of God
By Dr. Hendrik J Vorster

Everyone desires to be known as a pleasant to be around with kind of person. This book helps you develop values towards such a godly character. This book explores 52 Values of the Kingdom of God.

Books are available from our website: www.churchplantinginstitute.com

SPIRITUAL
DISCIPLINES
OF THE
KINGDOM
OF
GOD

Spiritual Disciplines of the Kingdom of God
By Dr. Hendrik J Vorster

Every Believer desires to be a Fruit-producing branch in the Vineyard of our Lord. Developing spiritual disciplines is to develop spiritual roots from which our faith can draw sap to grow strong and fruit-bearing branches. This Book explores Nine Spiritual Disciplines of the Kingdom of God.

Books are available from our website: www.churchplantinginstitute.com

Church Planting

How to plant a dynamic church

Dr. Hendrik J. Vorster

Foreword by: Dr. Yonggi Cho

Church Planting - by Dr Hendrik J Vorster

Church Planting - How to plant a dynamic, disciple-making church

By Dr Hendrik J Vorster

This is a handbook for those who wish to plant a disciple-making church. This book explores every aspect of church planting, and is widely used in over 70 Nations on 6 Continents. Here is a list of the areas that are explored:

1. The challenge to plant New Churches
2. Phases of Church Planting
3. Phase One of Church Planting - The Calling, Vision and Preparation Phase
4. The Call to Church Planting
5. Twelve Characteristics of Church Planting Leaders
6. Church Planting Terminology
7. Phase Two of Church Planting - Discipleship
8. The Process of Discipleship
9. Phase Three of Church Planting - Congregating the Discipleship Groups
10. Understanding Church Planting Finances
11. Understanding Church staff
12. Phase Four of Church Planting - Ministry development and Church Launching Phase
13. Understanding and Implementing Systems
14. Phase Five of Church Planting - Multiplication
15. Understanding the challenges in Church Planting
16. How to succeed in Church Planting
17. How to plant a House Church

Student Manuals and Video Teaching material are available from our website: www.churchplantinginstitute.com

NOTES

2. Walking with purpose

1. Online Merriam-Webster Dictionary word search.

6. Walking worthily

1. Biblehub.com, Strong's Greek Dictionary

www.ingramcontent.com/pod-product-compliance
Lightning Source LLC
Chambersburg PA
CBHW060349050426
42449CB00011B/2883